look at my eyes

look at my eyes

Autism Spectrum Disorders: Autism and PDD-NOS

Early Intervention and Navigating the System

melanie fowler

BCP

Look At My Eyes
Autism Spectrum Disorders: Autism and PDD-NOS
Early Intervention and Navigating the System

Brown Christian Press
A Division of Brown Books Publishing Group
16250 Knoll Trail Drive, Suite 205
Dallas, Texas 75248
www.brownbooks.com
(972) 381-0009

Serving with Excellence.™

ISBN 978-1-934812-98-3
Library of Congress Control Number 2011928036

Scripture quotations are from The Holy Bible, English Standard
Version® (ESV®), copyright © 2001 by Crossway, a publishing ministry
of Good News Publishers. Used by permission. All rights reserved.

Printed in the United States.
10 9 8 7 6 5 4 3 2 1

Author photos by Callie Shepherd, calliesheperd.com.

A portion of the proceeds from *Look At My Eyes* will go to
The Child Study Center in Fort Worth, Texas.

For more information, please visit LookAtMyEyes.com.

To my William
Who has given me a new life, perspective, and
purpose far richer than I deserve.

Thanks be to God!

In loving memory of
Mark Crawford Fowler
1947–2009

Loving husband, father, father-in-law, grandfather
"To all that is we say, 'thanks,' for all that
is to come we say, 'yes.'"

Go In/En Joy

Contents

Foreword

Autism is a pervasive developmental disorder. The word "pervasive" is used because the effects of autism pervade a large number of developmental domains including speech and language development, social development, emotional development, motor skill development, and academic skill development. In recent years, autism has become known as a spectrum disorder because of the variability with which its symptoms manifest in the various developmental domains across individuals. Indeed, children are like snowflakes—each is unique, and this is especially true for children with autism. Some may have a fully developed language repertoire but not have the social skills to make friends. Others may have high rates of verbal or manual stereotypes, but also have quite advanced academic skills. To be sure, an infinite number of gradations of behavioral excesses and deficits can be found across the autism spectrum.

Regardless of a child's "position" on the autism spectrum, progress can be made. All children can learn. Gone are the days when an autism diagnosis meant that a child would not learn to read, to play, or say "I love you." Today, the outlook is much brighter because of advances in medicine, applied behavior analysis, and speech/language pathology. Of course, the outcomes of even the very best evidence-based and scientifically-driven autism treatment are variable. These variable outcomes are due to a number of factors. Some of those factors include: (a) age of detection, (b) age at which treatment is started, (c) the degree of access to quality treatment, (d) the type of treatment delivered, (e) the amount of treatment delivered, (f) the degree of family participation in the treatment, and (g) the degree to which the child is delayed.

Daunting though the list of factors contributing to treatment outcome may seem, you must not let it paralyze you. Instead, use it to take action—to maximize your child's chances of the best possible outcome. All but the last factor are, to some extent, within your control. As such, if you suspect your child may be showing symptoms of autism, do not wait, do not let others assuage your worries by telling you, "He will grow out of it." Make an appointment with a neurodevelopmental pediatrician. If autism is ruled out, you will be relieved, but if it is confirmed, you will be one step closer to getting treatment.

If autism is confirmed, seek the services of a board certified behavior analyst with experience in the design and implementation of treatments for children with autism. These individuals can be found in autism treatment centers, in specialty private schools, and in private practices. In an effort to help parents evaluate the qualifications of behavior analysts who work with children with autism, the Autism Special Interest Group (SIG) of the Association for Behavior Analysis International (ABAI) has published *Consumer Guidelines for Identifying, Selecting, and Evaluating Behavior Analysts Working with Individuals with*

Autism Spectrum Disorders.[1] Make sure your child's behavior analyst meets the qualifications outlined in these guidelines.

Access to quality treatment is often influenced by geographical location and financial resources. Depending on where you live, you may have to travel long distances to reach high quality evidence-based services. You may also have to make some difficult financial decisions as you allocate resources toward treatment expenses. This, of course, will directly impact the amount of treatment that may be provided.

Finally, it is important to realize that family participation in treatment is critical to achieving the best possible outcome. Children with autism have significant skill deficits and although it may sound harsh, time waits for no one—not even children with autism. It is imperative that as much time as possible be used for therapy. Early intensive behavioral intervention by qualified professionals may be provided for up to eight hours per day. While this is a good start, this amount of time only covers a third of a day. Thus there are many more hours

1. Autism SIG Consumer Guidelines:
www.abainternational.org/Special_Interests/AutGuidelines.pdf

of the day open for additional teaching. Those families who receive training on how to become therapists themselves are able to arrange many more learning opportunities for a child with autism than families who do not get trained. The result of family training is better treatment outcome.

Look At My Eyes—universally recognized as a plea uttered by so many parents of children with autism is now the unforgettable title of Melanie Fowler's first book. The book highlights the importance of early autism diagnosis and treatment. Her message is clear and urgent: Do not wait. If you have a child with autism or you suspect your child has an autism spectrum disorder, the time to act is now. You will find Melanie's advocacy for early diagnosis and treatment to be practical and sensible. Moreover, Melanie's advice will help you avoid the unscrupulous charlatans peddling silver bullet treatments as she leads you straight to the evidence-based interventions that have been scientifically proven to produce meaningful outcomes. You will find yourself enamored by Melanie's passion, her courage, her conviction, her humility, and her humor.

Preface

The Group I Didn't Sign Up For

I didn't sign up for this. These concerns, these remarks and opinions, these lengthy—very lengthy—processes, this PDD-NOS—I didn't sign up for this. This was not my plan, not even close. But this plan became reality for me in the year 2005. If I was told, back when I first found out, that I would have to deal with all that I *have* dealt with, I would have said, "You're crazy! I can't and won't do it! I can't handle it!" And I would have said these things while burying my face in my arms, curled into a fetal position.

But the things I say today are different than the things I would say just a few years ago. Taking all my experiences into consideration, the things I would now tell my 2005 self—and anyone just beginning this journey—are things like, "Just because it is difficult doesn't mean you can't handle it, and just because you can handle it doesn't mean it isn't difficult." You see, handling any given situation on a particular day can mean many different things. For me, it can mean not losing patience with my son when he is asking me the same question hundreds and hundreds of times. Another day, it can mean just getting out of bed that morning when my son was up into the wee hours the night before. It can mean driving to another applied behavior analysis (ABA) therapy session that lasts three or more hours while juggling a one-year-old and talking to the insurance company about ABA coverage at the same time. If you're back where my 2005 self was, wondering how in the world you're going to cope, how you're going to handle the days and months and years of going through the same motions over and over, addressing the same problems over and over, it might help you to know that "handling it" will always mean different things on different days. You can't conquer autism in one day. You can chip away at it bit by bit.

I learned about "handling it" when I became a part of the group I didn't sign up for: the group of mothers of children with special needs. I think the first time I realized that I had become a member of the group was William's first day at the Jane Justin School. It was a special school designed to meet his individual needs, so perhaps I should have been feeling good about taking a tangible, positive step. But I didn't feel like that; I was completely and utterly depressed. I had done it. I had signed up. But I still didn't like what I was signing up for. Sure, it was a highly reputable school based on the science of applied behavior analysis, which I have come to greatly appreciate and respect, but I didn't *want* William to be different, much less be grouped in the same category as some of those other children. Why? Because it was a reminder for me that he had special needs. Looking back, I realize that I had a lot of learning to do!

Before William was born, I decided I wanted to stay home with him until he entered kindergarten. When he was diagnosed—at the age of two and a half—I still planned to take on the challenge and work with him at home. I wanted to do my best for him, but even more, I had a well-suited background for it. Looking back, I did accomplish enormous progress at home with William (with the help of professionals), but eventually I realized I could only do so much—especially with William growing older and another baby on the way. I knew William needed to be around other children. I needed to expose him to a social realm that I could only approximate at home.

Even knowing all those things, it wasn't easy. Initially, I cringed at the thought of my three-year-old going to an all-day school. It wasn't that I didn't think he would be receiving the best education possible—because I did. I was blessed to find a school so amazingly suited to his needs. No, I cringed at the feeling (rational or not) that a mother feels when she realizes, "I am not enough for my child." William needed more than I could give him, and he needed it now—hence the term "early intervention." I had to get past my own bitterness and disappointment at the situation and make his needs a priority over my feelings.

I hated feeling like he was "missing out" on his youth. What mother wants her child to be in school—not daycare, *school*—at the age of three? Probably all mothers feel something similar when their children go off to kindergarten, but this wasn't kindergarten and William was no five-year-old. But it needed to be done, for his sake. Early intervention is key.

At the end of the first day, a few mothers were waiting in line to pick up their children, and one, whose name I learned was Heidi, began a conversation with me. The first questions were the standard questions exchanged between all mothers, especially on the first day of school: "How old is your child?" "Is this your first year?" It wasn't long, though, before the questions became those that only members of this group, this club, would understand. We began talking about therapies and diagnoses, a conversation common to all parents of children with special needs, and that was when I knew for sure: whether or not I'd signed up for the group, I was in it.

Desperate to convince myself that I *could* handle this, I remember thinking, "This mother does it. How does she do it with such determination and strength?" I had not yet been exposed to the big shocker. Just as our conversation had reached a lull, the classroom door opened again. Two boys ran up to Heidi, grinning and showing her pictures they'd made at school that day. She had twins! Yes, twin five-year-old boys, both with autism spectrum disorders. Watching the two of them run up to her with open arms of excitement, my eyes began to fill up with tears, and it was hard work not to completely lose it. There I was, feeling depressed and anxious, and she had two dear, sweet boys in need of her constant attention. Though I had degrees and extensive training, Heidi taught me novels of information in just that five minutes of conversation and watching her with her boys. I vowed never to let autism overwhelm me or my family to the point where we thought that we had lost the battle or that we were missing out on something better for all of us.

After getting William settled into his carseat and climbing in myself, I closed the car door that day knowing things were different. I couldn't stop thinking about that mother and her two little boys, and I cried in the car as I thought, *Nothing will ever be the same. And actually, I hope that's the case.*

Even feeling as discouraged as I was on my son's first day of school, Heidi had given me hope and encouragement by her example alone. Today, her boys are seven years old and she continues to be an example and an encourager for me—she has energy and joy, and she shares it.

Over the following weeks, I began to identify with many of the mothers I met at school, with their hopes and fears so similar to my own. Socialization for William had been one of my main goals when I put him in the school; little did I know how much positive and much-needed socialization I myself would receive, too! I remember observing one particular mother and the way she delivered such grace, beauty, patience (lots of patience), and love to her special child. Even though she always had a lot going on with her autistic child and her other, younger child, she was incredibly patient and positive. After having the privilege of getting to know her, I realized that it was her faith that allowed her to remain composed as she tirelessly pursued autism treatment. She was a calm person, even in chaos. She knew the Lord had given her this situation. She was learning and taking it all in stride. Her attitude was amazing: Our children (angels, as she called them) are given to us by God, and it is a blessing to care for them. I knew that, and my little blessing was right in front of me the whole time. But sometimes the everyday struggles can really drag you down and make you forget the most important things. I just needed a reminder. I needed this group, and they needed me, too.

I think back to what we as a family went through before reaching the Jane Justin School. The private therapies, the conversations, the work—work at home with William, work in therapy—the everyday struggle, William's struggle, my daughter's struggle, my personal struggle, my husband's struggle. This all had meaning. Even those early days of school were tough: Besides my own conflicting feelings about putting William in school at such a young age, by the time he finished school at three in the afternoon, he was exhausted and grumpy. But putting our feelings aside and being proactive by putting William in school turned out to be one of the best things we did for our entire family. We soon found out that not only was he being exposed to other children in a social environment, he was learning to read. William began reading by the time he was four years old. That first year in school for William was such an eye-opener for me; I couldn't believe how much I was learning about him. He was also fully potty-trained by the first year, and that was a huge marker for us. In the year and a half since we joined the school, we've gotten and stayed involved, and it's made all the difference. Instead of sitting around feeling like there's nothing we can do, we get involved with the school and that gives us things to do, which helps us in how we face autism on a daily basis. Not only that, being involved has made us feel like a part of a huge family. Even though I hadn't signed up for it, I now am so grateful to be a part of this group—a group that nurtures, is helpful, and is honest (sometimes brutally honest)—the group of people who are looking out for their best interest as well as your best interest.

Looking around at all of these women, I realized that we are all a part of the group. No one who's a member discusses being a part of this group of extremely strong women; though we do lift each other up in difficult times, we don't sit around congratulating each other on how strong we are. We do what we must; we acquire the strength; it just becomes a fact of life. The membership, the strength, is implied every time we glance each other's way, catch a conversation before rushing off to conquer the day, or, in my case, get a little faith and brutal honesty shoved our way. This group allowed me some perspective, too. Sometimes when I look back at some of the things I've been able to survive and accomplish (through conversations with these ladies and my own quiet introspection) I'm shocked. It's not pride; it comes from the Lord—a feeling of thanksgiving for the strength that came, seemingly unbidden, when it was most needed. You will be surprised at what you can endure . . . what you can accomplish . . . and what your child can achieve.

Acknowledgments

I would first like to thank close family and friends who have given tremendous emotional and physical support when it was most needed.

I would specifically like to thank Vincent and Debby James, Bonnie Fowler, Elizabeth and John Baldwin, Paul and Melissa Russell, Brittany and Michael Norman, Frank and Judy Norman, Nana and Papa Bates, Cindy Campbell, the Baker family, the Penshorn family, David and Megan Skeels, Kris and Kelly Calvert, Ben and Gail Dyess, the Young Punk Breakfast Bunch, and the Moms' Prayer Group.

A special thank you to the Child Study Center and Autism Services Department, the Jane Justin School at the Child Study Center, ABA Academy, *FortWorthChild* magazine, Friedman, Suder & Cooke Law Firm, Fort Worth Presbyterian Church, Early Childhood Intervention of Fort

Worth, the Seay Foundation, Uplyft Creative, the Village Homes, V Fine Homes, and HD Homes Family.

A special thanks to Dr. Joyce Mauk for helping to improve the lives of the children at the Child Study Center so that they may achieve their full potential.

Thank you to Dr. Anthony Cammilleri, who strives to understand and teach my son to reach his full potential. He wouldn't be who he is today without your expertise, patience, and friendship. This book would not be in the condition that it is in without your knowledge and guidance.

Thank you to Michele Gortney, who provided me with much needed emotional support and encouragement during the early years of navigating through diagnosis and treatment.

And lastly, to my husband, who provides me with unwavering daily support. You are a true blessing and the more challenges we endure, the more I love you. It is by God's grace, mercy, and love that we are a team, determined to accomplish His plan for us according to His purpose.

Introduction

Early diagnosis and intervention is the key to success with any special-needs child. "My child doesn't need therapy." "He will grow out of this." "She is just different and unique, that's all." These are thoughts and rationalizations that every parent makes when sensing that something about their child is not "typical," and they were sentences that I thought and said aloud when waiting for my son to learn to speak. By the time I had William, I had earned a bachelor's degree in speech-language pathology and a master's in special education, specializing in deaf education. I was certified as an educational diagnostician and had spent years teaching children of varying ages, including teaching three- and four-year-old deaf children and teaching sign language as a foreign language to high school students. I'd been involved in a program as an inclusion specialist, working with children with autism spectrum disorders (ASD) who'd been mainstreamed into typical classroom settings. I had also done one-on-one home-based intervention with a severely autistic child using sign language. I had all that experience, and I still had these thoughts. Too often as parents we second-guess ourselves and don't trust our intuition, even when we really feel something might not be right. You need to act on these senses for the sake of your child's progress. Sounds a bit harsh, but it is true. You are actually delaying the overall progress your child could be experiencing if you sit and wait for other people to make decisions. There's one important key you need to know: reputable therapy will not hurt your child, it will only help. In the end, if your child ultimately ends up with no serious diagnosis, the therapy you allowed your child to experience will not have hurt him/ her. For example, my two-year-old little girl is quite verbal; actually, she is amazingly verbal. She always has been. Does she need speech therapy? No, but would it hurt her if she had it? Certainly not. In fact, I perform speech therapy strategies on her every day!

"But I don't want my child to have a label."
"I don't want the diagnosis at such young age."
Here's another bit of good news for parents
who fear the label: you don't necessarily need it
for early intervention. I'll explain more about
that in the next couple of chapters. If you are
questioning any type of behavior in your child,
why not take that leap and call a professional? I
don't mean just your pediatrician. There are many
interventions available, some at almost no cost to
you, as early as birth. Yes, really, from birth.

When William was diagnosed with PDD-
NOS (pervasive developmental disorder—not
otherwise specified), I had no time to read any
book over a thumbnail thick. I can't tell you how
many books are stacked up in a corner just sitting
there untouched—even now, five years later! I
needed something helpful and informative, but
it also had to be short, concise, to the point, and
hands-on. I needed *this* book and *these* words, so
I am giving them to you.

Seth Says…

What is different about this book versus all the
other books on autism that flood the shelves of the

local bookstores? Why do we need another book that describes the plight of a family struggling with having an autistic child? There are hundreds and thousands of books, blogs, videos, and papers about autism.

Parents with a child with autism don't have time to read, nor do they *want* to read a five-hundred-page book on autism; they're living the book minute-by-minute.

Much of the literature on autism is preoccupied with supposed causes and controversies.

You must put your energy into how you are going to help your child at this moment, but searching for ways to do that so often turns up a lot of research and even finger-pointing that, unfortunately, can't help you now. Your questions are a lot more pressing: "OK, my child has an autism spectrum disorder; what do I do next? How can I help my child now? What therapies are available for my child to receive?"

This book will help you through the beginning processes of grief, intervention, therapy options, helpful strategies in the home, and insurance coverage, and will give you more of an understanding of your role as a parent. My husband, Seth, has contributed throughout the book in the "Seth Says . . . " sections—offering thoughts, feelings, and advice from the perspective of a dad to a child on the autism spectrum. Whether you come from a traditional or untraditional family, if you're perhaps a single parent whose parents or friends or ex-in-laws are your sole means of support, whatever your situation is, I'm convinced you'll find that parenting one of these special children is really a team effort. We have certainly found it to be. Whoever your teammate is—whether it's your spouse, your ex, a teacher, a wonderful friend, your sibling, or your own parent—Seth's viewpoint, not only as William's dad but as *my main support system*, is sure to offer wisdom that can help you navigate this journey. You have a lot of work ahead of you and so this book is meant to be short and to-the-point. You don't have time to fixate on all of the possible reasons of why or how this happened. There are way too many, I promise, and none of them will seem like reason enough, anyway. Your world is changing fast, so let's get started.

one

So I Have a Concern: What to Do Next?

I can do all things
through him who strengthens me.
—*Philippians 4:13*

"Cold" was William's first word, spoken at fourteen months. I remember standing in front of the refrigerator, gazing over at William toddling nearby, thinking how funny it was that he chose that to be his first word. It *was* cold with the refrigerator door open, but hadn't we been going over, "The cow says *moo*!" and "The dog says *woof*!" about a trillion times? How often had I even said the word "cold" to William? Not very. Yet that was the word he spoke first. At the time I thought it odd, but also, like any parent, I was pleased. In fact, because I'd noticed his speech was delayed, I felt like we'd made a huge breakthrough; now he would start talking and everything would be OK. But by sixteen months, I knew his language was not progressing or functioning like his same-aged peers; he could learn new words but then might only say them once every three weeks or so. We had made a breakthrough, just not quite the breakthrough I'd thought at the time. And it was not just his expressive language that concerned me; I had a little list of things in my mind, steadily growing. By the time William was seventeen months old, I didn't want to wait any longer, so I called Early Childhood Intervention (ECI) in Texas, an organization I was familiar with because of my work before William was born. Every state has a different name for this type of service, so because the service is local to you, you must look into this. You can find the name of your specific program by searching on the Autism Speaks website. This local program provides children up to three years of age with a plethora of services, including speech therapy, occupational therapy, and physical therapy. Did you catch that? It means if you are questioning your child's development even the tiniest bit, you have a local organization that can help. These professionals will come to your house to assess your child to see if there is a need for their services. If there is a need, they will find it. The assessments are thorough. Your child doesn't have to be diagnosed in order to receive services through this particular program. When they have determined a need, you begin to receive services. I cannot say enough about the early intervention program that is near you. Sign up for as much as they will give you; it will be one of the most important service programs offered to you during your journey. It is affordable, based on a sliding scale, and run by qualified professionals in your home, helping both you and your child. Take advantage.

What we found when ECI came to assess William was what I already knew: his speech was developmentally delayed. But hearing it from an outside, objective person—someone who was trained to assess such things and who was not as emotionally compromised and as worried as I was—made me begin to pay attention to the other things I'd noticed. Other concerns on my list also began to grow: lack of eye contact, hand flapping, and weak recognition of his surroundings. We started receiving services right away, without a formal diagnosis, which was a relief because I really wasn't ready to have to cope with that possibility yet.

Our local zero- to three-year program provided us with tremendous support. Why? One reason is because I asked for it. When it was determined that he would receive services, I asked for everything under the sun and more. When they began meeting with William once a week for speech therapy, I called to get two days a week. Guess what? They provided it. If you want to get the most out of a service, don't be afraid to ask for what you want; it just might be available. You are your child's advocate, so ask questions, take notes, ask more questions, and be persistent—but remember to mind your manners. You want these professionals to respect you, and yelling or demanding will only lead to suffering and disappointment for everyone involved. My motto: ask for something with a grin and composed disposition.

There are so many issues in dealing with a child with expressive language delays. What could it be? Is it just a language delay that can be fixed with the help of speech therapy?

The first thing we did after contacting ECI and recognizing the language delay was a hearing test. If your child has an expressive language delay, I strongly recommend having a hearing test done first. The child of a friend of mine had a language delay and was put in countless therapies, yet was not making adequate progress. The child's hearing was finally tested and it was discovered that the child did indeed suffer from hearing loss. Not only did the mother suffer severe distress over not testing her child sooner, but the child also suffered much distress and frustration before the real problem was discovered. Lesson learned: get a hearing test!

I remember being in the testing room with William as he passed each test perfectly and seeing the look on the audiologist's face that labeled me an "over-worried mother." Even though I was almost certain William didn't have any type of hearing loss, I had to be sure before I moved on to therapy after therapy. So after he passed with perfect hearing, we moved on to the next logical question: if he could hear perfectly, then why did he act like he couldn't sometimes, and why was my list of concerns growing?

two

Diagnosis and
Early Intervention

But one thing I do: forgetting what lies behind
and straining forward to what lies ahead.
—*Philippians 3:13*

Even though I knew William needed special intervention, I still prayed every night that I was just an over-worried mother, like the audiologist seemed to think I was. I remember the day that changed everything. William was in the playroom focusing intensely on his cars and I got right behind him and clanged a spoon loudly against a pan. He did not even flinch. He was completely focused on his toys and totally unaware of his surroundings. That was the moment for me. That incident, combined with all of my other concerns, finally gave me eyes to see. I trudged back into the living room, sat down, and wept. I didn't want it to be true. But more importantly, I knew that I had to be seriously proactive.

Seth Says…

You have to throw out your expectations. "He's a chip off the old block." "Apple doesn't fall far from the tree." "Like father, like son." "Spitting image." I would wager that all fathers, when they find out they're going to have sons, immediately start setting expectations for their boys: "He's going to play quarterback for the Texas Longhorns." Or, "I can't wait to put a golf club in his hands." Or, "I'm going to teach him how to ride a horse better than I can." Whatever the father is into, he wants his son to be into it as well—and he wants his boy to be even better at it than he was or is.

Fathers feel as if they're going to be judged on how well they teach their sons to shoot a basketball, dress a deer, or know all the colleges of every NFL football player, and when the realization of having a child with autism hits you, as a father you experience a huge sense of loss. You feel depressed that you won't have a shot at teaching your boy how to tie a fly, throw a perfect spiral, or hit a perfect drive down the middle of the fairway. If you have a daughter, the heartache is still there. You may grieve less the lost opportunity to teach her to play football, but you will grieve just the same. You'll grieve teaching her to drive someday; you may even grieve the chance to chase the boys away as she grows older.

It's a father's right to be a peewee league football or softball coach, you think, *isn't it?*

It's not fun when a father realizes that he more than likely won't be able to live vicariously through his son because of his son's special needs. It's not pleasant for a father to realize that his son probably will never make the winning shot as the buzzer sounds—or even want to be around those types of settings. It's depressing and absolutely crushing, not only because we fathers are grieving for all the things our children will not experience, but because we are trained that it's a rite of passage to pass along our interests, desires, and skills to our kids . . . and that's probably not going to happen.

9

The faster a father can let go of those expectations, the better it will be for everyone involved—his wife, his child, his other children, and himself.

I grieved, am grieving, and will grieve—it is cyclical. To be the best advocate for your child, you need to keep going. You can do both—you will have to. Are you going to do it on your own? Absolutely not; you need the support of family and friends and qualified professionals. You need to open yourself up, even while grieving, so that you can learn more about how to help your child. There were days, many days, when I didn't want to even get out of bed. You have to grieve, and it is a natural process that will change over time. We will discuss in more detail the understanding of grief and the daily coping process that will follow in the next chapter.

After the incident with the pan and the spoon—after the day I *knew*—my husband and I decided to take William to see a developmental pediatrician. We found one by asking our regular pediatrician for a list of autism specialists. Autism specialists have a wide range of titles, but some include "developmental pediatrician" and "pediatric neurologist." If your own pediatrician does not feel it is necessary to make that call and you feel that you need more answers to questions relating to your child's development, then you need to make the call, without a referral, and take that initial step yourself. Don't second-guess yourself; if you have concerns, it's better to address them and be wrong than to ignore them and find out later your concerns were legitimate. Just pick up the phone and ask for an appointment. Do it soon because the wait list may be long. If it is long, get on the cancellation list and call incessantly to get in sooner than the scheduled date. It's OK to be persistent; in fact, it is crucial.

During our initial visit with the developmental pediatrician, I had notes, lots of notes, specific to William and my observations of him. Make notes, lists, whatever you need, and take them with you to see specialists and doctors—the whole process can be quite overwhelming, and if you don't have it all written down in front of you, you'll forget to mention or ask about important things. You need to know your child and how he responds to his environment well so that you can answer questions to the best of your ability. The more you know, the more specific help you will receive. I had a lot of questions, too. I had written them all down and my list was lengthy. We went through every single one. Ask as many questions as you want—really, you have every right. After answering my questions and discussing my son's whole life in a nutshell, the developmental pediatrician told me that she believed William did indeed have PDD-NOS. What does this really mean to you, though, if your child is diagnosed with PDD-NOS? You often hear about autism, but not as much about PDD-NOS. It means that your child has a few characteristics of autism but not enough to be diagnosed with the classic term "autism." It's a catchall diagnosis, used when the classic characteristics of autism are not all present. Healthcare providers may not provide a diagnosis of PDD-NOS until after they've considered all the other "types" of autism; in short, they may arrive at their conclusion after what is essentially a process of elimination.

Is it better to be labeled with PDD-NOS rather than with autism? Not necessarily—it is simply what your child is exhibiting at that particular time in his life. Children change; developmentally, any child can exhibit more or fewer characteristics over time. That could work in your favor, too. If you're feeling particularly disheartened by a diagnosis or the seemingly limitless mountain you have before you to climb, keep in mind that a diagnosis or label is not a death sentence—children absolutely change as they grow, and some children may exhibit more "typical" and less "autistic" behavior as they get older.

You may be thinking, *Oh, but I don't want my child to be labeled.* I understand that, but get over it. If the label means getting the help you need for your child sooner, then I am all for it. Make it work for you. If insurance coverage is an aim for you in trying to get therapy services covered, you will need a diagnosis—it will be impossible to get coverage without a formal diagnosis. Your child doesn't have to go around the rest of his life wearing a sandwich board that says "Autistic" or "PDD-NOS." No one is going to brand him.

And most importantly, there's no reason for the quality of your child's life, or his successes and failures, to be dictated by this label unless you want them to be.

As I've mentioned before, you might get by without a formal diagnosis or "label" for a while. During our time at ECI, a formal diagnosis wasn't even necessary for intervention. They simply came to my home, assessed, made recommendations for types of therapy needed, and began the process. It wasn't until William was two and a half years old that he was formally diagnosed and by that time, he was receiving many beneficial services. But I'll say it again: When the time comes that a formal diagnosis is needed in order to procure services or to get insurance coverage for something your child needs, don't balk at the idea. It's just a step in the process of helping your son or daughter.

three

Grief, Support, and the Big Picture

Blessed is the man who remains steadfast
under trial, for when he has stood the test he
will receive the crown of life.

—*James 1:12*

Like other parents with children on the spectrum, you will face many challenges, starting with the incomprehension and insensitivity of others unfamiliar with your situation. They may think your child is "misbehaving" and consequently deem you a parent unable to "control" him. This may be especially true if your child is closer to the PDD-NOS end of the spectrum, because PDD-NOS kids don't always fit into the more easily identifiable categories of autism spectrum disorders.

On the other hand, if your child behaves more like his "typical" same-aged peers when he is in public, you might find that others are quick to brush aside your concerns or your situation altogether. Even after he was formally diagnosed, sometimes I would discuss one of William's behaviors with a mother of "typical" children, and she would rush to assure me that, "Oh, my son/daughter does the exact same thing; that's normal."

This reaction is sometimes the most difficult to deal with. After all, I realize these mothers are trying to comfort or soothe me by convincing me that my child is normal, but the fact remains that William is *not* typical, as much as I might wish otherwise. If he is exhibiting normal behaviors, he's doing so as a result of *hours* or *days* of intensive work and therapy. Also, I don't want pity or a handout from these women—I am not seeking reassurance that my child is normal. It would be so much better if they responded with empathy and understanding rather than attempts to invalidate what I know to be true.

I cannot express to you how much you need and will continue to need support. You need help so that you have enough energy to be your child's advocate. Get your sleep any way you can. You need sleep or you will go insane . . . I speak from experience. Take shifts with your spouse or other support person and work out some type of schedule, especially when times are tough. Being sleep-deprived or stretched too thin is only going to cost you patience and quality time with your child, and neither of you stand to gain when you're at your mental, physical, or emotional limit.

Some days will be harder than others. The days that are "good" will give you patience and energy for the difficult ones. You will get breaks—there will be good days—so if you're in a "bad" day, just keep in mind that tomorrow might be totally different. We try not to take the good days for granted because we know they are precious ones.

In William's early years, I used to go into the garage and scream as loud as I could just to get the frustration out. It is terribly difficult and challenging not to fully understand what your child wants or needs. The lack of language can take a toll on the whole family. Believe me, there is no one on this planet who loves my son more than I do—only God loves him more—but there were and are times when I just wanted everything to disappear.

I am a believer in Christ and take comfort in knowing that he loves my son even more than I do, and that he created him perfectly in his eyes. William was not given to us by chance. In the past four years, my husband and I have learned to work together as a team and have dealt with the exhausting, difficult challenges that have faced our whole family. I can promise that you will learn an enormous amount of patience that you never even knew existed inside of you. The way you deal with challenges will change over time and you will grow to become more and more comfortable and confident in dealing with concerns and behaviors that arise on a daily basis. Situations arise every day that are new to you, and you will constantly work on how to shift, modify, and discipline any unwanted behaviors. While every day brings something new and different with children with autism, you will feel like you'll never become a natural because each day presents new challenges. I can assure you that it will and does get easier over time. You come to learn your own strength and know the depth of your reserves of patience and love, and all of those things help make it easier as you go.

As important as it is to have energy to work with these precious children, you also need time away to recharge. Seriously, part of your journey in learning how to help your child is learning how to help yourself—how to balance the never-ending quest for your child's wellness and development with your own self-care. Again, you can't be much of an advocate for your child if you never have time to regroup or recharge.

Besides making some quiet time for yourself once in a while, make time for your spouse. Even on days when you're exhausted and you have date night scheduled but you don't really want to keep that date, you need to do it. At least half the time, you won't feel up to it. But keep your date with your spouse anyway. It's important for both of you. It's a good way to talk about something else and to reclaim your other roles: spouse, friend, lover. If you don't have family or close friends nearby to watch the kids for a few hours, look to the church. Call around to different colleges and ask for students who are getting degrees in special education or applied behavior analysis. A social worker also has excellent community connections. It can be a great way to find a competent babysitter for a special-needs child. Don't let faraway family or unavailable friends keep you from prioritizing your marriage.

Seth Says…

Here's a brief tip for fathers out there with a special-needs child: get away! Seriously, marriage is tough and tiring enough with "typical" children; multiply that by thousands when dealing with a special-needs child. You've got to have time for one another.

One thing Melanie and I have started doing is dropping the kids off with friends or family and just getting away for a night. If that's not feasible for you, that's OK too. It doesn't have to even be an overnight event; spend the ten dollars an hour for a babysitter and go to the bookstore, go get a cup of coffee or a drink at the local watering hole, have a nice dinner, see a movie, be with one another—you need it.

I think this is good advice for all husbands and wives, not just those with special-needs children. If you don't take a few moments to spend together, then it's not going to last. Maybe you'll be able to skate by for a few months or years, but in the end, not taking time out to be with one another will doom your marriage.

Find a support group or create your own! When William turned three and became a student at the Jane Justin School, the first thing I did was create a moms' group. We met for coffee once a month after dropping our kids off at school at 8:15, and we discussed anything and everything—it was a safe place. Usually we met for an hour or two, and while it was a great time to pump more experienced moms for information, it was also just a blessing to be able to spend some quality time with a group of strong, inspiring women. This is no time to shut out friends or family or to hide. You must find a few friends that can care for your child while you take a little time for yourself. These people will be your outlet to sanity.

Seth Says...

One of the greatest blessings in my life since William was born is that I meet with a few buddies every Friday morning at 7:15 (well, some of us show up at 7:15) for breakfast. I learned this ritual from my dad, who would gather with his buds from time-to-time at a certain location to meet and talk and be there for each other.

Men don't get this opportunity very often these days . . . shame on us!

I value my wife tremendously. We need to be on the same team to make a marriage and family with a special-needs child work. She is a pillar of strength and feistiness. But I need to get away. We all need a break—even if we don't have a special-needs child.

I started having breakfast with buddies even before Melanie and I were married. It's just a good time of fellowship and cutting up and creating strong relationships with other men. Sometimes our get-togethers are about *Seinfeld* episodes, sometimes they're about work-related stuff, sometimes they're about issues at home, and sometimes they're just tears and nothing else.

Fathers with special-needs children need to find an outlet like this. If you don't have some sort of outlet—friends who you can just talk to without the fear of coming across as a horrible person—then you will explode and it won't be pretty.

I can't imagine not having my Friday Breakfast Bunch. When we started, one of the wives called it "Young Punks Breakfast" because her husband was one of the older members of the group. Now we're just the "Breakfast Bunch" because, while we're still probably all punks in some way, shape, or form (especially yours truly), we're not really classified under the "young" moniker anymore. Oh well.

Men, especially fathers with special-needs children: find a group that you can talk to, that you can confide in, that you can grow and really share with. It's not a substitute for your wife by any means, but there are times when you just need another buddy to talk to and your wife might not take it the way you mean it, or maybe you need to filter something past your buddies before you share it with your wife. Maybe you want to let off some steam without adding more weight to her shoulders. One way or another, you're going to need some supportive friends.

When a tantrum evolves into something larger and more complicated due to the lack of verbal expression and comprehension in your child, you will be challenged to your limit to make decisions that will be right for your child and for your entire family. It is hard, hard work to juggle the needs of all the people you love, especially when those needs seem to conflict. A small child already requires some serious multitasking skills; a special-needs child can really put your work ethic to the test. So again, let me stress: you cannot do this alone—it is too big and too overwhelming even for the most organized, motivated, multitasking, loving, and devoted mother out there. You need professionals who you can trust and family and friends to support you.

Daily prayer and support from a church community can also be very helpful and invigorating. I've heard numerous moms say that they tried church, even churches with special-needs ministries, and were asked to leave due to their children speaking out as a result of the noise or otherwise causing an interruption or disruption. No church should behave that way. My advice is: find another church! Don't cheat yourself and your family out of such an important and revitalizing resource—you will be passing up valuable support if you do. Go out and find a church that's better suited to your needs; you'll need the reinforcement and the companionship at some point.

I am not painting a clear picture if I don't include the many blessings that come as part of parenting a special-needs child. Of course there are blessings. We are constantly laughing with joy at the things William says and does and the tone is one of celebration, because we know that he has worked hard to progress day by day. PDD-NOS does not define who my son is; it is simply a characteristic that he possesses. William is a lover, a creator, and a builder. He is delightfully refreshing and honest. He is sensitive and remembers everything. He has a dry sense of humor that can make your concerned heart and soul burst into sheer laughter. He is my son, with or without PDD-NOS.

Seth Says...

I'm not saying it's easy or that the sorrow automatically goes away, because it doesn't. It will always pain me to think that my son might not ever want to see the Texas Longhorns play a football game, or that he might never be able to sit still and be attentive enough to watch *Star Wars* for the first time. It flat rips my heart out. But I love my boy. I'm proud of my son. No, he might not be something that I would have chosen, but he's mine and will always be my boy and my pride and joy. I crave for my expectations to be fulfilled, but some of them might never be. And as soon as I accepted that—as soon as I told myself to get over it—I noticed a difference in my relationship with him.

So he's not going to be the starting point guard for the San Antonio Spurs. He might never play organized sports of any kind, and I'm OK with that—I have to be OK with that. But you never know . . . maybe he will be really good at something that interests me . . . maybe I will have the opportunity to teach him something that I know a lot about . . . maybe we will go to New York City one day and see Broadway shows just like my father did with me. If that day comes, then I will be so pumped up and filled with joy. And if that day doesn't come, I still am pumped up and filled with joy that I have my son and he has my name and it's not about me or my silly expectations—it's about loving a child who isn't "typical" but who *is* a special child of God and someone I am proud of.

four

Setting the Bar High

Be strong and courageous. Do not fear or
be in dread of them, for it is the Lord your God
who goes with you. It is the Lord who goes before
you. . . . he will not leave you or forsake you.
Do not fear or be dismayed.
—*Deuteronomy 31:6, 8*

E very day is a new day. A new day for you to start over, a new day for you to work with your child, a new day for you to love your child and accept the unchanging while challenging your child to grow and progress at the same time. It takes strength and wisdom to know the difference.

As you may already know, every child with any type of pervasive developmental disorder is different. Each child possesses different qualities that make her unique to the spectrum. Some of your challenges will be completely different from the challenges of others, while some will seem quite similar. The worst thing you can do is to give up and think that your child has no chance. Every child will make progress when given the chance. That progress might not be exactly what you were hoping for or it may take a very different form from what you expected, but it is still progress. I remember working with a child with severe autism who was nonverbal while I was pregnant with William. She had no words to express herself and no one had even thought of teaching her sign language. She learned to sign more than twenty words within the first two months I began working with her. Never underestimate. They can and will rise to certain expectations that you have for them.

I have three important rules that I remind myself of daily when working with my son:

Rule #1: Just because you have a child with autism or PDD-NOS does not mean that every action they perform is due to their autism or PDD-NOS. Children simply disobey and have tantrums at times, and that is a natural part of the growth process due to immaturity and sometimes even simple exhaustion. We used to think that every time William had a "meltdown," it was because of his PDD-NOS. I learned better, though, and now I don't buy into that—and why should I? I am ecstatic to know that he exhibits some "typical" behavior similar to that of his same-aged peers.

Rule #2: Doing everything you can to help your child does not mean it should consume your every thought. You have a life outside of helping your child. Some of you reading are wives to your husbands, husbands to your wives, and mothers and fathers to other children. You may also be a friend, a sibling, a daughter or son, or an employee. At home, there needs to be constant open discussion about how to tweak and change situations for the better for the whole family and not just for your one special child. Not only is communication healthy in your marriage, but it is essential to the survival of your marriage. Some statistics go as far as to say that 80 percent of marriages with an autistic child will result in divorce. Whatever the percentage is, the odds are against us. Communication is a necessity, and if your needs and the needs of your spouse are not met, you will begin to pull apart.

Rule #3: It is important that you continue to set the standard high for your child while dealing with the daily challenges that you will face. I am a firm believer that setting the standards high can not only nurture your child but can deliver confidence, praise, and a desire in that child to perform and live up to those standards. Now, the steps to overcoming the challenges on the way to reaching those standards may not look the same as they would in other, "typical" children, but the concept is very much the same. No child should be underestimated. Set the bar high so that no barriers exist between where your child is now and where she could be in time.

These three rules help me to stay on track and to keep William and his struggles in perspective. At no time should his issues overshadow the needs of the family as a whole, and at no time should his status as a special-needs child afford him the right to endless bad behavior. If we accepted every negative and unwanted behavior of William's, he would be an entirely different child today. I do struggle with accepting his present "unchanging behaviors"—those behaviors that aren't going to change today or even tomorrow—but I have learned that even some of those behaviors can be changed or modified over time. The steps are slower when working with those kinds of behaviors, and sometimes those steps take us in a completely different direction than I had ever thought we would go, but progress is progress however you look at it.

It took us years to potty-train William. Those were really some of the nightmare times, because one of his habits was to smear feces all over his bedroom walls and furniture. I'm a clean freak and I would try to watch him every second, but he was very fast. Sometimes, an hour after we'd put him to bed, I'd go in to check on him, and the odor would greet me in the dark as soon as I tiptoed into the room. We tried everything but none of it made a difference. Even my screaming and crying and anger didn't affect him; within minutes he'd be staring off into the distance and giggling. I took many, many trips out to the garage, where I would stand and scream in frustration just to let some of it out. But I had to remind myself that it was not personal: pouring all my anger and my frustration into my child was pointless, and the attention may have even served as an unintended reinforcer.

Besides being immune to my anger or sternness, William, like many children with ASD, has a high threshold for pain. Physical discipline in any situation for William was useless. In the stage at which he made a habit of spreading feces all over the walls and into the carpet, he would "do his deed," get a reprimand, and then do it again thirty minutes later. What finally did work was a removal of privileges, but we tried so many things before we found that solution. I am fully convinced that if we had not pushed, persevered, and gone a little crazy and creative at times, he would still be in diapers, spreading feces all over the walls. My point is, you cannot give up and think, *This is it; it will never change.* If you do, it is certain to remain the same. So how do you figure out when and where to push your child and when and where to accept? You love your child; you're motivated by love; and of course you want her to be as healthy and accomplished as possible. But where is that invisible line, and how do you find it? First, and I know this sounds cliché, I would advise you to take it a day at a time. Accept the things you cannot change on a daily basis. Slow down and calmly tell yourself, "OK, he cannot do this today but maybe he can tomorrow." Don't look too far into the future in ruling out the things that you feel your child will never be able to accomplish. It's as simple as that. I don't know what William will be capable of five years from now, but I do have an idea of what I would like for him to accomplish in that time frame. That is the big difference between accepting the temporary "unchanging" events and accepting that your child will never learn something altogether. I choose to do the former.

Another facet of the "one day at a time" rule is daily observation and time spent with your child. I knew William had the potential to overcome many obstacles and challenges simply by observing him at home. He understood much of what I said to him and could follow simple instructions. This gave me some leverage to work with him more intensely. For example, I figured that if he can put toys into a box, then why can't I teach him to clean up after playtime? Before I knew it, he was doing it! Finding time and putting the effort into having your child build up to that desirable behavior or skill is crucial for the success of your child. Performing "hand-over-hand" activities early on can lead to independence later. You place your hands over your child's and you do the action for him, but he still has to participate. You do this until you can begin to taper off your own action or participation little by little, until finally your child has reached his goal independently and without your help. For more information on this and other important teaching techniques, contact a board certified behavior analyst. You see, you must set them up for success and not just expect them to one day "get it." It takes time to bring about change, but by using the guidelines and methods presented in the following chapters, you will be on your way to seeing progress in your own home and not just with a therapist in a formal setting.

How else do you find that line for your child? Getting an outside opinion from those who worked with William proved to be extremely useful in helping him realize his true potential. I tapped the experience of professionals outside of my own area of expertise. I had his IQ and achievement levels tested. This gave me a lot of information to build on. Every child has the potential to succeed and make developmental progress—and children with autism are no exception. This might be the hardest thing for you to hear if you're still grieving your child's diagnosis: "assuming" that a diagnosis of autism is a death sentence of sorts is going to hold your child back more than the autism itself, most likely. You *must* confront and deal with those feelings, because your child will need you to push him to be better and to have faith that he can be.

Seth Says...

Discipline is something that I have really struggled with in the more than five years we have had William. I was not raised with a heavy hand at all, but I certainly believe and subscribe to the principle that no matter what age you are, there are consequences to your actions and behaviors.

I have always believed that parents should give their children more credit than they do and realize that their children know what right and wrong are from an early age. If they are taught that there are un-fun consequences to poor decisions and behaviors, then they will learn from that—remember, children are sponges. Bad behavior = discipline. I would say that's a pretty standard school of thought for most parents.

But what about when you have a child with autism? Then you can pretty much throw that philosophy out the window.

Children with autism don't process situations like typical children. They don't see things like you do. Things are not always black and white or linear or so basic to them. You have to realize that oftentimes, your child is reliving certain situations for the first time. For example: hot stove, curious child; child touches hot stove; child burns hand; child cries in pain; therefore child has learned not to touch hot stove.

Oh, if it were only that simple for children on the spectrum! With some children with autism, it's more like this: hot stove, curious child; child touches hot stove; child burns hand; child cries in pain; child does it again the next day.

So here's the advice: be consistent with the consequences. If you're going to discipline your child for doing something once, stick with it and discipline him every time he makes that poor choice. Be patient. Your child is not processing as you would process. Your child might not be able to put together the scenario of making a poor choice and suffering a consequence as a result. Don't baby your child. The sooner he realizes the relationship between his actions and consequences—whether good or bad—the better. The goal is for your child to be as self-sustaining as possible one day. If he doesn't learn about actions and consequences at an early age, then how disadvantaged is he going to be in the "real world"?

I'm sure some parents would disagree with me. They would tell me that their child doesn't understand what's going on and that I'm cruel and unjust in my viewpoint. OK, I'm not saying I'm an expert or that I have it completely figured out. But I'd ask those parents this: If you don't think your child can learn the relationship between negative actions and consequences, then how come he can understand the relationship between positive actions and consequences? If my son will sit down in a chair at the dinner table and eat his food because he sees that there's a treat at the end of the meal, then he can also understand that if he keeps getting out of his chair and putting food on the floor then he will be guided to comply.

Be patient. Be consistent. Be fair. Be willing to try new things . . . because you'll try them all and then some.

I have had many people ask me, "Is it difficult accepting William for who he is?" Today, I simply reply with, "Yes." Then I go on to explain that I strive to accept the present unwanted behaviors today but will persevere that much more tomorrow in working for that desired behavior.

In the beginning when I heard the word "acceptance," it just seemed like a word for giving up and not finishing the race. It took me a long time to understand what "acceptance" really meant for me and my family. Yes, it is difficult when I cannot be in complete control of William's daily and present progression. Yes, I would love for him to overcome obstacles faster than he sometimes does. But what I do know is that my son is fully capable of overcoming great obstacles, and there is so much more he and I have left to do! So there is that balance of acceptance and the never-ending desire to continue to push and strive for continued success.

five

Look At My Eyes

I have no greater joy than to hear that my
children are walking in the truth.

—*3 John 1:4*

Having a child with an autism spectrum disorder can present daily challenges. Many of these come from the child, but you'll find that well-meaning friends, family, and others can certainly contribute to what is already a difficult situation. This happens a lot before your child is diagnosed and may happen even afterward, especially if your child, like William, sometimes exhibits a few of the "classic" autism traits. People who do not know your child may not even notice that he is not typical.

Children with autism, to those who are unfamiliar with autism spectrum disorders, can seem standoffish, uncaring, disrespectful, or even rude. This can be a difficult thing to deal with in social settings. There are certain behaviors that we expect of one another, and when those behaviors are not offered or exhibited, our first impression is usually one of rudeness. Eye contact is something that most of us take for granted—we even expect it from small children—and it has been one of our greater hurdles with William.

In the early years of William's life—actually even as early as nine months old—I noticed that William seldom made eye contact with us. But I assumed that eye contact was something you had to *teach* to your child. Especially since William was my first, I didn't know any better; I just thought that every milestone took work. It was only after I had Margaret that I realized how easy it is for typical children to engage in using eye contact. By that time, of course, William had been diagnosed with PDD-NOS.

There was a time before we realized what the problem was when we would say William's name over and over again in the hopes of getting his attention, getting him to look at us. But when he was diagnosed, we were told to be very specific with him—to tell him exactly what we wanted him to do. So, instead of saying "William!" and expecting him to immediately look at my face, as my daughter does when I call out her name, I learned to instruct him: "Look at my eyes."

Eye contact was never easy for William, but we soon realized that if he wasn't exhibiting eye contact with us, then it would be even more difficult to teach him to do so with others . . . and he had a lot of learning to do. So even now, every day, my husband and I say to William, "Look at my eyes." This helps him to focus and "watch" the words come out of our mouths. It organizes his "next steps" when he is able to make eye contact. Not only is eye contact crucial for social engagement and acceptance, it is necessary in teaching rules, consequences, and facial expressions and cues. I can tell William to put his shoes on a hundred times, but if he is not looking at my eyes and reading my cues when

I ask him, he usually won't do it. Most of the time, I have to tell him to look at my eyes and then I give the instruction. Right away, he will respond with either a yes or no. That may not sound like an ideal reaction to an instruction, but either way, it is a response, and it's better than what I'd get *without* eye contact: no verbal response and no action at all.

In the beginning, it was hard to stop everything and have to ask William to look at my eyes all the time, but I knew from experience that if I didn't, the outcome would not only be confusing for William, it would also be frustrating for all of us. There are mornings when we are on our way out the door for school, rushing because we are running late, and I realize that William has not put his shoes on. I have to stop what I am doing, go to him (kneeling down), and say, "Look at my eyes." Then when I have his attention, I can tell him, "Put on your shoes now," and he complies. Your phrasing may be a bit different, but we have always stuck with "Look at my eyes."

You will have to stop what you are doing often to go through this process with your child (the kneeling, the repetition, etc.)—maybe even hundreds of times a day if you are working with your child at home. Is it an inconvenience for you? Sure, it seems that way at times, but if you don't do it, your child will never reach his full potential. Remember also that your child will exhibit in public the behavior that you have taught him at home.

I wanted William to say hello and make eye contact with others—that is important for social engagement and growth. It didn't take long for family and friends to catch on that I meant business in this department. In the beginning, we were met with, "Oh, that's OK, he doesn't have to look at me." Or, "Don't worry about it; he doesn't have to say hello." I would say, "No, he does. This is a part of his therapy and he is expected to give greetings and eye contact, even for a split second, because it is crucial to his growth and development." Or I would reassure them, "You are helping him to grow and progress if you ask these things of him." Will he get it right all of the time? No, but he will become more and more comfortable in looking at and speaking to others, and that is progress.

Don't be afraid to keep demanding that your child establish eye contact with you and others, or that he keep interacting in general, even if you notice it makes him uncomfortable. You see, it's not that you are "being mean" as a parent; you are actually being a supportive advocate for your child.

six

The Nitty-Gritty: Hands-On Strategies and Helpful Hints

For this commandment that I command you today
is not too hard for you, neither is it far off.
—*Deuteronomy 30:11*

Children can become very frustrated when they have no language and have no way to express wants and needs. First thing, how can we give them a way to tell us what they want and need that is more graceful rather than having a tantrum?

Seth Says...

"If you don't do something for your child with autism, then no one is going to do it for you." Those were the words that hit me like a cold splash of water as we sat in an all-day autism conference that I didn't want to attend. Filled with anger, bitterness, frustration, and sadness, I had been sitting in the "Dads Only" breakout session, which had only about seven dads in attendance, when I heard those words.

"If I don't make the effort to get my four-year-old child with autism involved in the 'typical world,' then he will become yet another autistic statistic and slip through the cracks," I told myself, "and that's not going to happen!"

That was in June 2009. From that day on, I had a totally different perspective, attitude, and drive to be a part of my son's life and to never stop, never quit, and never look back when it came to dealing with his diagnosis. I would never let his label prevent him from doing whatever he wanted or anything that a "typical child" could do.

I remember attending an autism conference in Texas with my husband. There were so many parents there with specific questions about how to help their children, and although I personally appreciated the theory and background of strategies presented by knowledgeable professionals, I left thinking, *These parents need more.* You need basic instructions and examples to help get you started. I have put together scenarios and examples of ways in which parents have dealt with challenging times. Again, not all children with autism are the same and their challenges differ in many ways—you'll have to figure out what works for your family. But these examples are ones based on applied behavior analysis, which have worked for families I have known and in my own home, as well.

Sign Language

Teaching sign language to children with autism may be a good option for those who need a non-verbal language for long-term communication or as a transition to verbal speech.

The practice of signing is effective because it is visual and many children quickly adapt to the language. Signing with your child can teach language as well as improve communication and social skills and it may also help to lessen undesirable behavior, such as tantrums or biting.

Contrary to what some believe, sign language actually stimulates rather than inhibits verbal speech and language development in some children.

PECS

Picture Exchange Communication System (PECS), developed by Andrew Bondy and Lori Frost, is a system for helping children with delays in speech development to communicate. For example, the child is given photo cards depicting his favorite toys. When he hands a card to a parent or other communication partner, the parent then hands the toy to the child. In this way, the child begins to understand the importance and rewards of communicating, and hopefully will then be more motivated to pursue speech.

PECS is amazing and science-based. Even if your child has pretty good expressive language, a visual can be so helpful. For example, William can label almost anything if you point to it and ask him, "What is that?" but getting him to understand that he must get dressed in the morning to go to school became such a struggle. The screams and the tantrums almost became unbearable before I thought to create some visuals—cards showing drawings of his clothes. The visuals completely calmed him and put things in order for him, and he felt like he had some control. Then I was able to direct the getting-ready process like this: "William, it is time to get ready for school. Do you want to put your pants on first or your shirt?" There I would hold up the two cards, one for pants and one for a shirt. He was able to make choices on his own, and before he knew it, he was dressed. And it was accomplished with less strain and resistance, leading to a better outcome and easier mornings.

Use pictures to help your child visualize as many concepts as she needs. You will know when you need to use the cards—your child will let you know, not always in a subtle manner. Related to this are activity schedules, developed by Krantz and McClannahan. Activity schedules are a sequence of visual cues, such as pictures or photos, which help a child with autism complete complex tasks or series of tasks or activities independently.

Not an artist? You can find free black-and-white PECS pictures online. Cut them out, laminate them, buy some Velcro and a notebook binder, and you've got yourself a mobile pictorial system to take with you anywhere. Even if your child has words (as William did), extra visual cues help in explaining a situation and likely ease the anxiety and stress your child may be experiencing. Explaining a trip to the doctor, dentist, or even grandma's house by using pictures to help them see and understand what is going to happen next can make a huge difference in the ease of daily activities, for both your child and you. When you see your child come unglued because of a slight transition, delay, or change of schedule, a PECS system created for and modeled after your own schedule use can be very helpful.

In general, many children with autism can do well with either sign language or visual communication techniques such as the Picture Exchange Communication System (PECS). Children who are learning to speak verbally may find signing a helpful transition to verbal speech. Some children with more severe cases of autism may prefer PECS to signing because of the visual aids.

Parents should seek the advice of a licensed speech-language therapist to help figure out which nonverbal language works best for their child.

Behavior Management Strategies

Understanding what motivates your child's behavior and deciding how to approach it can be a daunting task. There are some general and effective strategies to consider as a starting point. It is important to individualize them for your child. Some of these techniques—positive reinforcement and planned ignoring—are straightforward in theory, but may prove to be difficult to implement. Try to remember to set reasonable expectations for yourself and your child and seek the support of a trained board certified behavior analyst (BCBA).

Differential Reinforcement

Children typically enjoy receiving attention. If they do not receive enough positive attention for their good behaviors, they will often resort to less desirable forms of behavior. If you attend to those undesirable forms and ignore the good behavior your child will quickly learn to behave poorly. On the other hand, if you attend to the good behavior and ignore the poor behavior, you will get more good behavior and less poor behavior. Over time, children learn which actions are the most effective in getting your attention. So the choice is yours. You can attend to the good behavior and get more of it or you can attend to the bad behavior and ensure more struggles. Attention is powerful. It can be used to share both good and bad behavior. Be careful how you attend to your child.

It is important to show your child more attention for acting appropriately than for acting inappropriately. This will help motivate them to continue behaving appropriately. When used along with procedures to reduce inappropriate behaviors, such as ignoring (see below), it will encourage your child to display behaviors that will gain your approval. It is important for children to learn that only appropriate behavior receives your attention.

Differential attention requires you to attend to some behavior (good) and to ignore the other behavior (bad). When used correctly, your child learns inappropriate behaviors result in no attention and acceptable behaviors result in lots of attention. It may sound simple, but implementing this procedure with precision can be difficult. Nonetheless, its power to shape behavior can not be overstated.

Giving attention effectively:

- **Make eye contact with your child and speak enthusiastically.**
- **Be specific about the behavior that you liked.**

    For instance, "Good being quiet," or, "Nice hands to self," instead of "Good girl."

- **Keep praise statements simple**

    For instance, "Good picking up toys," instead of "That was good picking up your toys so that no one would trip on them."

- **Give attention during or immediately following the behavior you like.**

Delays in attention (or any reward) make it less effective as a reinforcer for a particular behavior.

- **Give the type of attention that your child enjoys.**

   All children have their preferences. Make note of the type of attention your child enjoys. It may be different from what you enjoy or what most children enjoy. It is important that the attention you use to reward appropriate behavior is truly a reward to them. If not, it won't work as a reinforcer.

- **Catch your child being good.**

   All gains and appropriate behaviors are important and should result in positive attention. Statements such as, "Nice sitting on the toilet," or, "Nice brushing teeth," are important for your child to hear.

- **Provide lots of attention for behavior that is incompatible with inappropriate behavior.**

   Example 1: If your child flaps his hands while walking down the hall, teach him to put his hands in his pockets. Keeping hands in his pockets is incompatible with flapping and should earn lots of attention.

Example 2: If your child sucks his thumb, teach him to chew gum. Chewing gum is incompatible with sucking a thumb and is also more socially acceptable.

- **Be sure that good behaviors receive more attention than inappropriate behaviors.**

Provide many opportunities for positive attention.

It is easier to promote appropriate behaviors when your child is doing something she likes to do and you are both focused on that one activity (instead of cooking dinner or folding laundry while your child plays). The more you arrange the environment to be conducive to appropriate behavior the better the chance your child will learn how to act appropriately.

Get in the habit of catching good behavior and providing positive attention at least once every five minutes. You will know you are praising your child enough when you feel you are doing it too much or too often.

Using Planned Ignoring

Determine what is "ignorable behavior." Ignorable behavior is typically defined as behaviors that are not harmful to the child, others, or others' belongings. It is important that all family members and caregivers be aware of the definition to be consistent in their response.

- **Ignore as soon as the behavior occurs.** Planning to ignore attention-maintained problem behavior means that if the behavior occurs, you will not attend to it. In other words, you are going to make the behavior nonfunctional with respect to attention.

- **Ignore consistently.** Whenever ignorable behaviors occur, consistently ignore. The best way for your child to learn the limits to her behavior and to determine which behaviors will result in attention is through consistency.

- **Make ignoring obvious.** To have an impact on behavior, your child must be aware that attention is being removed because of specific behaviors they have done. This is particularly challenging for children with autism who are less aware of social cues. Therefore, ignoring must be made obvious by looking away, keeping a neutral facial expression, talking with others in the child's presence, restricting physical contact, or engaging in household tasks.

- **Expect behaviors to escalate.** Things often get worse before they get better. This is because your child increases the frequency of behaviors to receive the attention she is accustomed for them. This does not mean that ignoring is not working. It is actually quite opposite, they are merely testing the new rules that have changed.

Escape Attenion

Do not allow your child to escape a task following problem behavior.

If you ask your child to complete a task, such as putting toys away, ensure that he completes the task. Do not allow a tantrum to let him to escape the task.

Ignoring is a very active strategy that requires that you withhold eye contact and make no verbal response to the child. However, it does not mean to stand back and allow destructive or other bad behavior to occur. It is important at times to prevent and block behaviors as well as remove or divert a child from an area or situation. It is important to keep everyone and everything safe.

The core to effective teaching and shaping appropriate behavior is *consistency, consistency,* and you got it, *consistency*!

- **Use eye contact.** Eye contact is a must for children with autism. When you are modeling eye contact while your child is talking, you are communicating that you are listening. By using eye contact when you are talking, you are showing your child that watching someone's face when they talk is important. Encourage eye contact; make your child work toward it. Eye contact is not especially easy for children with pervasive developmental disorders.

But if they have to look at you in order to get a certain special prize, such as a favorite food, playtime with special toys, etc., they will learn to use their eyes. It simply comes down to teaching.

- **Be face-to-face.** Try to position yourself at your child's eye level when possible. This models healthy eye contact and also demonstrates appropriate spatial proximity while talking with someone.

- **Speak in a natural, yet relaxed way.** There is no need to slow your speech to an atypical rate, but being very "relaxed" in your speech rate can be helpful. This conveys that you aren't in a rush and hopefully reduces the perceived sense of time pressure during daily activities (as compared to telling your child to "slow down").

Using Prompts to Teach New Skills

Children with autism may do better using specific teaching methods for new tasks. Your child must understand the request, what action to take to follow the direction, and then do those things. Teaching your child to follow simple instructions is a basic tool for managing your child's behavior. If your child is not attentive or receptive to your demands then this will limit your child's ability to learn more adaptive ways of responding.

One way to present new directions and teach the requested response is through using a procedure called graduated guidance. This method is effective with gaining compliance in most cases. There are three basic steps to the procedure:

Verbal prompt: Give your child a clear instruction and wait five seconds. If they follow your direction, praise them in a manner that specifically and concisely details what they did well. For example, "Good job putting on your shoes." If your child does not comply, move to the next step: a gestural and verbal prompt.

Model prompt: Show your child the exact response you desire. As soon as you complete the task, return things, or yourself, so they are exactly the same as before you gave the prompt. Say, "Now you do it." Wait five seconds without providing any other cues. If your child complies, praise them specifically for their actions. If they do not comply, move to the next step: a verbal prompt with physical prompt follow-through.

Physical prompt: Take your child hand-over-hand through the entire response as you say, "Please (repeat instruction)." This means you should be guiding both of your child's hands from behind the child. This is also called "hand-over-hand" guidance. No praise is provided if you must utilize this step.

The way you say things when talking to your child is very important. Your child is more likely to do what you ask if you avoid some common pitfalls of giving instruction. These include giving long or multiple requests at one time, providing vague requests such as "Be a good boy," issuing questions rather than statements (false questions), repeating instructions (nagging), giving instructions when there is not enough time or energy to follow through, and failing to achieve eye contact. Use one-step, concrete instructions as much as possible.

When using the physical prompt, it is important to demonstrate the exact response you want. This is where you are teaching your child what is expected. It is important to teach it correctly the first time. Initially, you may want to practice this prompt sequence within the context of one specific task (e.g., dressing, eating). That way, you can practice the sequence in a natural, time-limited situation and your child will master a new skill that makes life a little easier.

A few more tips:
- Establish a standard schedule and routines for your child. The more predictability your child has in her day, the less often you will need to guide her through specific tasks.
- Do not give an instruction unless you are willing to follow through with ensuring that your child complies with it.
- Set up situations so your child earns more attention for compliance than for noncompliance. Remember, it is going to take some practice.

Set Your Child Up For Success

In order to shape appropriate behaviors within your child, it is important to create opportunities in the environment for the behavior you want to occur. It is equally important to respond to inappropriate behaviors with effective management strategies. Below are some general guidelines that address both of these angles.

Note: A board certified behavior analyst will work with you and your family to build specific recommendations and plans for your child.

Do not set expectations too low. Your child *is* capable of learning. Rather than picking up skills naturally, many children with autism learn from explicit teachings. Regardless, your child will develop skills. Expect progress and growth.

Do not set expectations too high. Set realistic goals. It helps to break down tasks into separate steps that you prompt and respond to independently. This encourages success and reduces the stress or frustration.

Change activities often and always try to end with success. Just as it is important to set reasonable expectations, it is important to know when and how to end a teaching session or change activities. When you are teaching your child a new skill, take a break before your child becomes fatigued or frustrated and misbehavior arises. If possible, end the activity at a point where they have achieved some success and on a positive note. This will build your child's positive feelings about her abilities, and yours too.

Use things your child enjoys as reinforcement. When your child has done something that you want to encourage, it's important for them to see your response as a worthwhile reward. Keep in mind many children with autism may take particular pleasure from some things that others would not find particularly reinforcing or gain pleasure from. That's OK. What is important is that your child sees the reward as reinforcement for the behavior or work that has been done.

Allow *choices* whenever possible. Providing choices may help the situation without lowering your expectations. For example, if you would like your child to sit down, you can say, "Please sit down—do you want to sit in the big chair or the little chair?" Or, "It's time to get dressed—do you want to put on your pants or shirt first?"

Plan ahead for transitions. Children with autism tend to have difficulty with changes or new activities. You can help by allowing for adequate time and using prompts that are effective for your child about the change as it is about to occur. This may mean specific verbal cues, a visual schedule, or physical cues (a touch or gathering specific items) that communicate what is coming next.

Discipline

As I mentioned, for almost a year, on a daily basis, we would find William spreading feces on the walls, on the carpet, and on any furniture in his room. The carpet also reeked of urine. It is difficult to express how much distress this caused in our household. I described "screaming it out" in the garage, but even that doesn't do the situation justice, nor does it communicate the grueling cleaning and disinfecting that was an endless, constant chore in our lives for that year or so. It really was one of the most difficult times and challenges we have faced. And as I also mentioned, many children with autism do not connect physical discipline with the unwanted behavior—and in many instances it just makes things worse.

But we finally found something that worked for us in this situation: the removal of privileges. We knew that William loved to play with his Matchbox cars every day. One morning I walked into his room to find a feces mural all over the wall. I looked at him and said, "If you poop in your room, you lose your cars." I meant that he would lose them for a certain amount of time, but five minutes away from his cars was like an eternity for William.

Your own struggle might be different, but you'll have to try various things, like we did, before you find something that will work for you. And do not plan on everything changing overnight. For most children with autism, a slow progression is a blessing within itself. After we began to take his cars away as punishment for unwanted behavior, the occurrences came less and less. This meant more and more good behavior which, of course, earned his cars back.

Time-out can be very effective if used appropriately and consistently. Getting a timer is very smart as now the child's focus is on the timer and not on you for putting him in time-out. Once I set the timer for time-out, William will actually stay in the designated area until it goes off. You may need to guide your child the first few times, but he will begin to understand the drill. If hitting themselves or others is a problem, time-out can be effective. Your child should not have any type of engagement during time-out—no arguing, no talking. Time-out is supposed to be boring and non-stimulating. In fact, the phrase "time-out" is short for "time-out from positive reinforcement. You will know when it is working when the unwanted behaviors begin to dissipate. In order for time-out to be effective at reducing problem behavior, the "time-in" environment must be interesting, engaging, and full of positive reinforcement. If *not*, there will be no difference between the conditions and the behavior won't change.

When/If/Then Statements

I cannot end this chapter without talking about this. I literally use these statements with William every day. When/if/then statements are wonderfully effective, especially for children with some receptive and expressive verbal skills. They are helpful in breaking down steps, organizing thoughts, and may be coupled with PECS for additional support.

- Use "when" when you want him to do something.
- Use "if" if you do *not* want him to do something.

When/Then:

Child: "I want outside play."

Parent: "Put on your shoes, please."

Child: "No, I want outside play!" (Child begins to throw himself on the floor while screaming.)

Parent: "*When* you put on your shoes (use PECS here if needed), *then* you can go outside."

If/Then:

Child: (About to climb on the furniture.)
Parent: "*If* you climb on the furniture, then you will go to time-out."
Child: (About to throw food.)
Parent: "*If* you throw your food, then you will not have outside playtime."

Sounds simple and it is. It simply specifies the contingencies between behavior and the consequences of behavior. Being explicit with children with autism is indeed helpful! Again, every child is different, but the use of these statements has brought more peace into my home as well as a calmer and easier disposition within William in how he reacts to situations. In a sense, we simply specify the rules and we make sure everyone lives up to them. Following the rules produces pleasurable consequences, and not following them does not provide pleasurable consequences.

Seth Says...

For William's third birthday we got him a swing set. Not just swings, but swings, monkey bars, a climbing wall, a slide, a ladder, a rope ladder, and bars to hang from—it was amazing!

We got it for him because I pretty much got tired of hauling him to the park. We had a few neighborhood parks where we lived and we had a good time on Saturday mornings taking a ride in the red wagon down the block to the park. That part I didn't mind; in fact, I enjoyed pulling William in the wagon. He wouldn't talk or make much noise, but I would still talk to him. I would tell him about the homes we were passing and I would describe the materials or the architectural style of the homes, or I would comment on how pretty or ugly I thought the houses were. That part I enjoyed, maybe because I held out the hope that he would just "snap out of it" and say, "Gee, Dad, you're right, that soffit *is* painted the wrong color for a porch," or something like that.

What I got tired of was getting to the park and then him not wanting to play there. It was about ten blocks up and downhill, and I have to admit, I wasn't always doing it with a happy heart. We'd get there and he would just sit in the wagon or want to run away and I'd have to beg him to play at the park.

But when he did fixate on the park, it was always the swings. I swear, he would swing for hours if you would push him… and that's where I really got aggravated. I would start pushing him and he would say, "Go fast," or "Higher," and that's all he'd say for about ten minutes or more. Yes, I was grateful that my child was speaking, but I didn't want to hear "Go fast" or "Higher, higher, higher" for ten minutes at a time—this from a child who wouldn't respond to any of the other things I'd said to him.

Of course, my brilliant stroke of genius to get him a play yard for his birthday didn't change anything except the fact that I didn't get to comment on the neighborhood homes as we walked to the park. He still said "Go fast" or "Higher" constantly, and when I say "constantly," I do mean *constantly*!

I will teach him to swing for himself if it's the last thing I do. One day he will understand the concept of "Bend your knees, straighten your legs" that I have recited to him about a billion times to no avail. I can't wait for that day!

Or can I? Amidst all my angst and frustration about pulling him to the park, only for him not to want to go to the park, or pushing him for twenty minutes or more while he shrilled out one-word orders to me over and over and over… amidst all that, I have realized that we found a common ground.

I don't know if William will ever go to a game with me, or if I'll ever be able to take him to his first haircut, or if I'll ever build a model with him. But we found something to do together. We have our thing. It might not be fun all the time; in fact, sometimes it gets really tiresome, but you know, it's our thing. When the day comes that he learns to move his legs back and forth and doesn't need his daddy to make him go fast or go higher, it'll be a bittersweet moment for sure.

seven

~~~~~~><~~~~~

Beyond ECI:
Therapy Options

Now to him who is able to do far more abundantly
than all that we ask or think, according to the
power at work within us, to him be the glory.

—Ephesians 3:20-21

Before we "graduated" from ECI, our
local early intervention program, I was
working on what our next step would be. I
didn't want any time to pass in which William
wasn't receiving some type of help. When
you're trying to line up your next step or avoid
downtime, as I was, persistence is key. You have
to make calls, send letters, and get on waiting
lists, which can be quite lengthy. But try not
to let it overwhelm you. Another reason we

welcomed the "label" was because it helped us to center and focus in on what therapies would directly help William. Therapy can be expensive, and you must look at what you can receive from all different angles and price ranges. *More expensive does not always mean better;* your first and main decision will be choosing between private and public therapies.

There are a bountiful number of private therapies available—therapies focused on or specializing in almost anything. Look for evidence-based therapy like applied behavior analysis and speech therapy. Beware of quackery. By definition, a "charlatan" (also called a "swindler") is a person practicing quackery or some similar confidence trick in order to obtain money. Charlatans will tell you what you want to hear and promise the moon. Ask for data and proof; don't be gullible.

Just remember, driving from therapy to therapy can be exhausting for everyone in the family, and finding a therapy environment conducive to working on many facets of your child's development, rather than just one or two, is always a better choice when it's possible.

Free public school therapies may be available to children as early as the age of three. Call your local school district for more information on how to start the assessment process. Be prepared. Many schools will drag their feet because another diagnosis in the district means more money they have to spend. Some districts will use the assessments performed at your local early intervention program, but most won't and will want to perform their own assessments. This is a stall tactic so they don't have to spend money.

One of the most important parts of the special education process in a public school system is creating a plan for your child's education. This plan is called the Individualized Education Program, or the IEP. The IEP is the foundation for your child's education, and you are a very important member of the team. Your child's IEP lists the specific special education services your child will receive, based upon his individual needs. This is why it is so important that you understand and help develop your child's IEP. For more information regarding Individual Educational Programs, go to www.wrightslaw.com.

When considering your options, it is important to ask questions. This is a completely new domain for you, and you have every right to ask questions. Some questions you'll want to ask every therapist are:

- What are your credentials?
- Are you certified?
- What do you charge and can I see the breakdown?
- How do you note progress and can we set up meetings to discuss progress?

Keep a notebook of details on every therapy, therapist, and progressive step you would like your child to make. Keeping track of your goals for your child will help you to find a therapist who is like-minded.

The list of therapies for autism has grown extensively in recent years. You must make your own decision based on your own research, what you can afford, and how you can optimize each therapy to the fullest potential. The more people you talk to, the more options will come your way. Reject options without evidence of success. I'm talking about real evidence from science and not just testimonials. Whatever you choose, make sure you have done your research and feel confident in your decision. You should never choose an option out of fear. Especially watch out for the fear that if you don't do everything, you are not doing enough. That's an easy one to fall into, but it will only wear you out emotionally and physically.

Remember that a "one-size-fits-all" approach usually doesn't work for a child with autism; a multi-pronged regimen may be the most advisable. Below is a list of science-based therapies that may be of interest to you.

Applied Behavior Analysis (ABA)

ABA is widely recognized as the single most effective treatment for children with autism spectrum disorder and the only treatment shown to lead to substantial, lasting improvements in the lives of individuals with autism.

An ABA program is a systematic teaching approach that involves breaking down skills into small, easy-to-learn steps. Praise or other rewards are used to motivate the child, and progress is continuously measured so the teaching program can be adjusted as needed. Each ABA program is unique and tailored to fit your child's needs. Parental input and involvement in ABA is essential to the success of the child.

ABA is the only treatment for autism whose benefits have been consistently validated by independent scientific research. In fact, ABA has been endorsed as an effective intervention for autism by the American Academy of Pediatrics and the United States Surgeon General.

Note: Every child can benefit from ABA interventions by learning new skills and reducing problem behaviors. Seek a board certified behavior analyst (BCBA) when signing up for an ABA program, especially if you want insurance coverage.

Speech Therapy: Communication problems among children with autism vary to some degree and may depend on the intellectual and social development of the individual. Some may have well-developed vocabularies whereas others may be completely unable to speak. Therapy must begin with an individual assessment of the child's language abilities by a trained and licensed speech and language pathologist.

Occupational Therapy: Occupational therapists provide training in daily living skills such as dressing and hygiene, as well as fine motor skills related to holding objects, handwriting, cutting, and other activities. Their treatments rely on the use of specific tasks or goal-directed activities designed to improve the functional performance of an individual as it relates to the smaller muscle groups.

Medical Treatment: There is no medicine designed specifically for children with autism. You should talk with your developmental pediatrician for specific medicine that might be beneficial to your child's specific symptoms.

Fun Activities: There are a plethora of fun activities your child with autism can engage in, however, do not confuse these activities for legitimate therapies. For instance, William loves to ride a horse named "Charlie." Is it a therapy that will help cure his autism? No, but he likes riding and I enjoy watching him smile. He also likes kung fu and although I am ecstatic that William is learning right kicks, left kicks, and front rolls, it simply is not therapy; it is an activity that he enjoys.

Unfortunately, there are many doubtful or discredited methods available today that simply prey on parents of children with autism. Why? Because it is money in their pocket! Quack Watch, my favorite new website, focuses on health-related frauds, myths, fads, fallacies, and misconduct. Some discredited methods related to autism include chelation therapy, auditory integration therapy, and the use of hyperbaric oxygen. For more information regarding legitimate websites related to autism, please see chapter 9, Helpful Information.

eight

Insurance Companies and What They Don't Want You to Know

Trust in the Lord with all your heart… acknowledge him, and he will make straight your paths.

—Proverbs 3:5–6

Most children with autism spectrum disorders will need a combination of applied behavior analysis therapy and physical, occupational, or speech therapies. They may also need a psychological and medical consultation. If you feel that you have the right to insurance coverage based on your policy and you are running into obstacle after obstacle, consider resubmitting, following up on your claim, and even filing a grievance. If you are not getting the answers you want, call incessantly and don't take no for an answer. A good rule of thumb is to keep detailed records of *every* phone call (date, time, person's name, and what was discussed). One of the easiest ways to do this is to sit down at your computer before you make the call—that way, you can type notes into a document as you speak to the insurance company. Then all you have to do is hit "Save."

We certainly fought our insurance battles. We were denied many, many times—too many to try to count. Every time I called to check in about coverage and the lack thereof, I had to speak to a different person; I was never given an extension line. You see, that is exactly what they don't want you to have. It's quite ingenious, really. Every time I called, I had to speak to someone who didn't know my situation, and therefore I had to repeat the whole story. Naturally, the story got longer and longer every time I called. It was beyond frustrating, and going through that process affected me in ways that I can't even describe. But I somehow managed to stick with it, and every time I spoke to a different representative, I wrote it down.

Sometimes they were not polite; this kept me going, though, and helped to build a case—a good one. I can remember a specific incident when I called and spoke to a young man with no compassion or desire to help me in any way. I had just cleaned and fumigated William's entire room due to another episode of potty-training "noncompliance," and I was tired. It was only nine in the morning, and I already felt defeated. I called the insurance company knowing I would have to repeat my story and I was dreading it, but I wanted ABA therapy for William and needed coverage. After finally going through my spiel and realizing that I was getting nowhere— again—and that the representative was being rude, I began to lose it. I started crying and William was in the background screaming and spinning. I could barely hear the representative but I didn't care. I had no secrets. I finally said, "Well, I might just need to get a lawyer involved then." He said, "Ma'am, I wouldn't bother with that; it won't do you any good."

And in that moment, I knew I could win.

As a child, I never liked anyone telling me what I was or wasn't capable of doing. I looked down at William in that moment and thought, *I am not giving up on him and therefore won't give up on this!* For me, that was all it took. For someone on the other end of the line to act as if he had the right to dictate my son's future—never! That day, I was not defeated. That day was the beginning of triumph and perseverance.

As with many things, one of your best tools is knowledge.

Important facts to know about your plan:

- What is the in-network co-pay *or* what is the out-of-network co-pay?
- What is the percentage of reimbursement for in- and out-of-network providers?
- What are your in- and out-of-network deductibles?
- What is your out-of-pocket limit?
- What is the lifetime cap? What is the yearly limit?
- Is preauthorization or predetermination needed for out-of-network providers? If so, what is the submittal process?

Tips on how to get some help with coverage:

- Call the number on the back of your insurance card and ask for ABA coverage.
- Determine if you have ABA coverage under your major medical benefits and if not, ask about mental health benefits. Some companies will pay for ABA under mental health benefits.
- Once you determine coverage, ask how you get reimbursed for your ABA—most policies will have you pay out of pocket and then have you expense the claim.
- You will need to have the claim form and the Tax ID Number from the place where you are receiving ABA treatment.
- You will most likely need a letter from your developmental pediatrician with the Autism ICD9 code, which is 299.00.
- If needed, ask your company to provide out-of-network provider reimbursement forms.
- Never send originals; it is highly likely that your submittal may get "lost" in the shuffle.

Still getting nowhere? Get creative! With some insurance companies, almost any treatment billed to the insurance company with a diagnosis (ICD9) code of 299.0, 299.1, 299.8, or 299.9 will either be denied or limited. In that case, it is very important that you try to submit bills that charge for the symptoms you are actually treating, not autism. For example, many ASD children have gastrointestinal disorders, but you cannot submit a bill to the insurance company for the treatment of Gastroenteritis (ICD9 558) under ICD9 code 299, Autism. You must submit it under 558. Depending on the practice where your child is receiving care, you may be able to bill originally under the codes for the symptoms, or they may have a policy to bill under Autism and wait for a possible rejection before trying a different tactic. Work off the principle of billing for the symptoms you are actually treating. Think outside the "autism box."

You may end up needing to file an official appeal. First, you'll need to get your "ducks in a row," so to speak.

Information you will need for the appeal:

- Your health insurance plan
- The written denial
- Doctor/therapy bills
- Doctor's referrals and therapy prescriptions
- Medical records
- Physician's letter of medical necessity
- Study references that show the treatment works

Call the insurance company and confirm the denial and get reasoning. Take good notes and get names, phone numbers, extensions, etc. When filing a formal appeal, learn and follow the insurance company's guidelines and processes, and use the proper forms. If you don't follow the exact process, the claim will definitely come back marked "denied."

I grin when I think of our win against our insurance company. They finally listened and admitted to the wrongful denial. They were also held accountable for the hours of ABA therapy William did not receive while we were battling, and for the speech therapy for which they had refused to pay. Yes, it took time, lots of time, but we are not "special cases" as the insurance companies would have us believe. You can fight, too, for the same results—it is possible to triumph, with perseverance and a little feistiness.

If your insurance is not paying attention to you and is denying every claim, but money is an issue as it was for us, don't give up. There are still a few ways to get your point across. You may want to find a lawyer friend, or friend of a friend, or just any lawyer who is willing to write a letter at a small charge. This is to get their attention, to let them know that you are not going away. Such a letter may expedite the process and may cut through the delay tactics of your insurance company. If not, maybe the lawyer would be willing to take your case to the next level in the hopes that the attorney's fees will be paid for by the "opposing team." We didn't have the money to pay attorney's fees, but our lawyer took a risk on us and we won—after eighteen months of fighting. It never hurts to ask for help, and you will find that there are many people willing to give it.

Remember, "autism" is unfortunately still a buzz word. Insurance plans are beginning to listen, but you have to be willing to fight to the end. Most insurance companies want you to give up and go away; that is why they deny your claims. You can send everything they need for approval and they will still try to find loopholes to get out of paying. That is just the way it works.

nine

Helpful Sites

Ask, and it will be given to you; seek, and you will
find; knock, and it will be opened to you.
—*Matthew 7:7*

Since autism was first identified, there has
been a long history of failed treatments and
fads. History has been dominated by improbable
theories about causation and treatments.
Many of these treatments have been too
quickly adopted by professionals, too readily
sensationalized by the media, and too hastily
embraced by hopeful consumers—well before
supporting evidence or reasonable probability
existed for their effectiveness or safety.

Type "autism" into any search engine and you will find millions of references. Before you begin surfing the web at three o'clock in the morning, check out these top sites. All of them are science-based, readable, and contain links to many specialized services and related organizations.

Association for Behavior Analysis International

www.abainternational.org

The Association for Behavior Analysis International (ABAI) is a nonprofit membership organization with the mission to contribute to the well-being of society by developing, enhancing, and supporting the growth and vitality of the science of behavior analysis through research, education, and practice.

Autism Special Interest Group

www.autismppppsig.org

Aside from educating parents about behavior analysis, the SIG's other primary initiative is helping parent attendees get the most out of ABAI and its conferences. The PPP SIG provides information, networking, and resources for these parents.

The Association for Science in Autism Treatment

www.asatonline.org

Their mission is to share accurate, scientifically sound information about autism and treatments for autism. Here you can read about autism treatments, descriptions, and research summaries for psychological, educational, and therapeutic interventions.

Behavior Analyst Certification Board

www.bacb.com

Looking for a board certified behavior analyst? Look no further. This website will provide you with a list of certified analysts in your area.

Autism Speaks

www.autismspeaks.org

This site has some of the best resources, including links to local chapter websites that provide specific local information (like how to find your local ECI program). The section titled "Autism and Your Family" has wonderful advice, and the section titled "Your Child's Rights" has a description of the services your child is entitled to under the law. Autism Speaks provides a valuable tool, *First 100 Days*, an eBook that helps parents organize themselves in the first one hundred days after receiving the diagnosis of autism.

Child Study Center

www.cscfw.org

The Child Study Center (CSC) provides diagnosis and treatment services to children who have, or are at risk for, developmental disabilities and related behavioral and emotional problems so that these children may achieve their full potential.

Jane Justin School

www.cscfw.org/School/tabid/70/Default. aspx

The Jane Justin School, in partnership with families and the community, fosters the knowledge and life skills necessary for students to achieve productive and meaningful lives while respecting and embracing the individuality of each child. Their goal is to one day be able to return their students to traditional educational settings with the skills needed to be successful in those settings. The Jane Justin School accomplishes this goal through the use of cutting-edge, evidence-based, and scientifically proven teaching techniques.

Quack Watch

www.quackwatch.org

Quack Watch provides information regarding health fraud and quackery. Autism Watch specifically provides scientific analysis of therapies related to autism as well as provides reliable sources of help and information. It is also here where the unreliable sources are identified.

ten

In-Home Activities

There is nothing better for a person than that he
should eat and drink and find enjoyment in his toil.
This also, I saw, is from the hand of God.

—Ecclesiastes 2:24

This is a list of suggested supplies that can
be used in your home to implement skills
such as language, sensory, fine motor and gross
motor, and daily living/self-help.

Language Skill Supplies

- Letters of the alphabet/Leap Frog Fridge
  Phonics
- Numbers
- Touch and feel books by DK Publishing
- Coloring books

- Creative play scenes (farm, school, doctor/nurse, birthday party, train station)
- Toy phone and camera
- Puzzles
- Activity picture cards
- Play food
- Shape sorters
- Puppets
- Age-appropriate board games (Twister, Candy Land, memory cards)
- Felt storyboards

Sensory Skill Supplies

- Play-Doh
- Bubbles
- Bath foamies
- Crafts (stickers, feathers, pom-poms, etc.)
- Beanbags
- Musical instruments
- Play food
- Shaving cream
- Finger and sponge paint
- Stamps
- Sand toys
- Squishy balls

Fine Motor Skill Supplies

- Tool box or work bench
- Stacking toys
- Squishy balls
- Dress-up clothing
- Lacing pictures or beads
- Blocks
- Finger and sponge paint
- Child scissors
- Snap beads and toys
- Puzzles that involve zippers, snaps, laces, latches (Check out Melissa and Doug puzzles.)
- Crayons
- Wipe/erase boards

Gross Motor Skill Supplies

- Plastic balls
- Kickballs
- Basketballs
- Child bowling ball set
- Beanbags
- Mini trampoline
- Large building blocks
- Slides

- Tunnels
- Hula-Hoops

Daily Living/Self-Help Skill Supplies

- Pots and pans
- Tub toys: foam letters, numbers, shapes, and animals
- Melissa and Doug supplies: Shoe Lace Puzzle, Pizza and Cookie Set, and Basic Skills Board
- Plastic food
- Toothbrush, wash towels, comb, brush, etc. (to use on dolls for visual learning)
- Costumes for imaginative play
- Toy phone
- Play house: people figurines and play furniture
- Dolls with snaps, zippers, and Velcro

How do I use these items at home to engage my child?

Try using one or two items per skill subgroup listed above each day, and then decide which activities and items are best suited for you and your child. The items listed are to help guide you into a well-orchestrated at-home therapy program for you and your child. It's like your own therapy session right at home, and you and your child can have fun while learning!

Below is a list of activities to get you started in using the items listed above in each skill subgroup. I use these fun activities with William at home, not to take the place of outside therapy programs, but to be used in conjunction with and as a supplement to these programs. Each activity will provide you with lots of fun with language for you and your child. Choose a few to do each day and you will begin to gain knowledge of your child's favorite activities as well as her areas of strength and weakness.

1. **Reading books:** This is a must! Reading to your child will help prepare him for listening activities and experiences in the classroom environment. Point to pictures and encourage your child to identify objects on the page. Name items on the page and have your child point to them and repeat the items named. Read a variety of touch and feel books. Name the

different textures, such as soft, slippery, rough, smooth, bumpy, and furry. Have your child say the word that is associated with the textures in the book.

2. **Word chart:** Make a word chart of all of the words your child knows how to say and put them in a visible place for him to view. I laminate cards with words that William knows how to say and I put Velcro on the back and attach them to a big felt board that I have in his room. We can take them on and off the board for continued use again and again. Add to the word chart with each new word that he learns how to say. You may also want to make a picture book of words he can say and have him point to each while naming the object.

3. **Sing-along songs:** Sing nursery rhyme songs, such as "The Wheels on the Bus," "If You're Happy and You Know It," "Row, Row, Row Your Boat," "Twinkle, Twinkle Little Star," and "Head, Shoulders, Knees, and Toes." Use hand gestures while you sing and help your child gesture by using hand-over-hand guidance.

4. **The shape sorter:** This is a great tool for many facets of your child's development. You can teach colors, shapes, and concepts such as "in" and "out" and "up" and "down." Say the name of the shape or color and have him pick it up and place into the correct slot, or have him say the shape or color and place the block into the correct slot.

5. **Puzzles:** You can't go wrong with puzzles! Use a variety to teach about objects, places, shapes, alphabet, numbers, colors, transportation, foods, and types of animals. Point to a puzzle piece and ask the child what it is a picture of. Respond by saying what it is and have your child repeat after you. If he is not talking yet, respond to your own question and use hand-over-hand guidance to help him put the puzzle piece into the correct slot.

6. **Toy animals:** Play animal sets come in all sorts of thematic scenes, such as farm, zoo, and pets at home. Teach your child the names of the animals and the sounds they make. Play "find the animal" and have him try to say the animal's name.

Have him point to the different animals and say their sounds.

7. **Flash cards:** Use a variety of flash cards of everyday objects at home and in nature, as well as animals, transportation, shapes, numbers, letters, and food. Have your child name the picture on the flashcard. If your child is not yet talking, name what the picture is and have him point to it. If he is talking, have him try to make a sentence about each picture or have him repeat a simple sentence, like, "The dog says *"ruff,"* or, "I want a cracker."

8. **Action cards:** Action cards are a good transition from one-word flash cards. Show pictures of everyday routines and play. Have your child describe what the child in the picture is doing. William first began this activity using only a one-word descriptor. We slowly began to stretch the response into more complete thoughts, for example, "What is the girl doing?" Answer: "Swing." With much practice and prompting, his answer transitioned to, "The girl swinging outside."

9. **Face cards:** You may also want to show cards with a variety of children's expressions, such as happy, sad, mad, and afraid. This will help your child to talk about different emotions and will build an awareness of how others may feel. "Do you think she is happy or sad?" Try to make the same emotional face that is on the card—get your child to mimic you if you can—and give an example of when one might feel that emotion.

10. **Felt storyboards:** One of my most favorite tools! Create imaginative stories and tales of different adventures. Identify and reposition all sorts of different objects as you tell your own stories.

11. **Go on a picnic:** Pack a picnic basket and have your child help with the items. Have them name each item as you pack for your adventure. Read a book about food items. While sitting down, have your child request the items that he wants: "I want juice," or "I want sandwich please."

12. **Play-Doh:** An old favorite, tried and true! Use Play-Doh and styling tools such as shape molds and cutters, a rolling

pin, etc. Have your child repeat words such as "roll," "squeeze," "push," "pull," "pat," and "poke." Ask him to name the color, shape, object, letter, or number he is creating.

13. **Odorless shaving cream:** Preschool teachers always have this item in stock in their classroom and for a very good reason—it is amazing, fun, quick, and easy to clean up! Spray shaving cream onto a table or placemat. Have the child press his fingers and palms into the shaving cream and play with it. You can draw or write letters or numbers, or make fun shapes in it. Lots of creative dialogue here!

14. **Bubbles, bubbles everywhere**: Blow lots of bubbles all around the child. Let him try to step on and pop the bubbles. Use words such as "pop," "touch," "clap," and "stomp" with your child.

15. **Sticker wall:** Place a variety of stickers in front of your child and ask him which sticker he wants to put on the wall first (use paper taped to a wall or over a table). Make collages or sort by color, animal,

shape, etc. Ask your child, "What is this a picture of?" Or, "Do you want me to put the sticker on your hand or arm?"

16. **Play food:** What a fun way to create all sorts of games and dialogues! Tell your child what each food item is and have him repeat the name. Put food in pretend pots and pans and use lids as well. Store the food in containers. Encourage your child to talk about each food item while he is playing. Ask all sorts of questions such as, "What color is this fruit?" "Do you want the peas or carrots?" Mix up the food items and tell your child to pick the food that you name. Ask him to pick a food that is red, yellow, or green. Play pretend restaurant and ask your child for a certain food and have him get it for you.

17. **Lacing beads:** Have your child string large wooden beads on a thick piece of string. Ask the child, "How many beads are on the string?" "What color beads did you use?" Have your child string beads to make a bracelet or necklace.

18. **Let's play ball:** Sit on the floor with your child in front of you. Roll the ball

to him and have him roll the ball back to you. Next, stand up with your child and gently toss the ball to him and have him try to catch it. Show him how to toss it back to you. Say, "Roll the ball," "Throw the ball," and "Catch the ball." Tell him to put his hands out so he can catch the ball. Bounce the ball and count the bounces together from one to ten.

19. **Body parts:** Teach all the different body parts. While standing in front of your child, touch a part of your body and have him copy you. Say, "Touch your head," "Touch your nose," "Touch your toes," "Clap your hands," "Wiggle your fingers," "Shake your head," etc. Sing "Head, Shoulders, Knees and Toes."

20. **Dressing up and down:** Naming clothing items is a wonderful act to practice during your child's daily dressing time. Practice in front of a mirror so that he is able to see himself. Allow your child to actively assist and provide hand-over-hand assistance only as needed. Encourage him to dress and undress himself to promote increased independence. Say, "Put on your underwear please." "Put on

your shorts/pants please." You may want to first lay out or spread out the underwear and shorts/pants on the floor so that he can sit down on the floor while putting each leg through the hole of the garment. Once this step is mastered, the next step would be to have your child practice standing up. This will promote balance as well as spatial reasoning.

21. **Photo books:** Use a camera to take photos of your child's favorite items, such as play toys, food items, family and friends, pets, etc. Laminate the photos and punch holes in the photo cards. Put a binder ring through each hole to make a book. Your child will love looking at photos related to his favorite things! This book will provide you with loads of language fun.

eleven

Looking Forward. And Back.

For you formed my inward parts; you knitted
me together in my mother's womb. I praise you,
for I am fearfully and wonderfully made.

—*Psalm 139:13–14*

William has come very far. So many of
the behaviors that seemed permanent
or irresolvable have been replaced with more
graceful responses. He's potty-trained, for
example. I don't just mean he's no longer
painting murals on the walls; he can now go to
the restroom by himself, wipe himself, pull up
his clothes (though, like many five-year-olds, he
needs help with snaps and buckles), and wash
and dry his hands afterward.

William has a higher than average IQ and is very smart; he can read paragraphs these days. Even more exciting to us, he's able to answer yes-or-no questions. Like many children on the spectrum, William suffered from echolalia, which means that often, when one of us would ask him a question (even something simple like, "Would you like some carrots?"), he didn't answer. Instead, he would compulsively repeat the question or the last few words of the question. "Like some carrots?" he would parrot. As of just a few months ago, though, he is now able to answer yes and no when I ask him simple, direct questions. It's amazing; a huge breakthrough. It took a long time. And even though yes and no are only brief responses, he's giving us conversation—he's having a dialogue and he's in our world. Those are certainly positive steps.

William had aversions to some foods because of texture; for example, he wouldn't eat pasta or applesauce for a long time. He's a fairly good eater now, though, and will even eat the foods he once avoided. He didn't really have any other issues with textures, but for years the sound of sirens—like those of an ambulance or fire truck—really freaked him out. He has learned to tolerate them now. Now we make it more of a friendly thing: "Hi, fire truck," we say, and then, "Bye-bye; fire truck all gone." This helps to remind him that yes, the annoying sound was or is here, but those sounds are going away now— no big deal.

As William grows and we never give up working with him, we have the joy and satisfaction of watching him overcome many challenges. Some will always be challenges, though, still things to work on in the weeks and months and years ahead. What's still really hard for William is being in large groups. He starts to flap his hands, jump, and ignore directions. At this age, I would love to take him to *The Nutcracker* for Christmas. However, having him walk beside me in large groups would be too difficult. He'd want to go somewhere he's not supposed to, I would refuse, and the situation would devolve into a tantrum. Birthdays are usually tough, too; he doesn't want to open gifts in front of others. Margaret's getting older and we want to participate in more activities and outings as a family, but some of those things we just can't do, so we've got to be creative about what we *can* do.

William does like being around others, his cousins, for instance. Not only that, but he exhibits more investment in those around him than he ever used to. He follows his older cousins around and wants to be with them, though he doesn't yet know how to interact with them gracefully. He also knows when someone has left the room, can verbalize accordingly, and cares that the person has left, whereas before it was questionable whether he even noticed. He can handle small groups and wants to be around small groups of family and friends.

Perhaps most important, he is building a relationship with Margaret, who is his younger sister by two years. He's learning to share with Margaret, and though his affection for her is sometimes hard to spot, I know they are figuring each other out. For example, they were sleeping in twin beds at my mother-in-law's house, when Margaret dropped her blanket on the floor in the dark and couldn't get to it and was crying. William got out of his bed, screaming, and headed for the door. We heard his screams and got there before he reached the door on his way to our bedroom. He wanted us to come and solve the problem for Margaret—even though he didn't know how to communicate that—so he did what he could.

William learns and exhibits new skills every day, as your child does or will, too, once you get started with her. I joke that William is my navigator; he knows how to get places and notices before I do if I've missed an exit. He doesn't tell me with words yet, but he does let me know in other ways. He can point out buildings he knows, can work on computers at school, and can even work a computer mouse.

Not everything is perfect. William is clumsy and needs to work on his gross motor skills, but he's come a long way. As a younger child, he was fairly inactive—he barely even crawled, preferring instead to scoot when he wanted to get somewhere. These days, though, he can do jumping jacks, ride a bike with training wheels, climb, and do a forward roll. It took him a long time to learn how to run, but he can do it now.

For William's future, I plan on social skills groups—perhaps by the time he gets to middle school. These are classes in which children learn social cues and basic conversational exercises. He's not ready for these types of classes yet; he doesn't have the comprehension. I envision him being typical in a lot of ways, but socially it's always going to be work for him. He's not likely to be outgoing or boisterous. That's OK—it's who he is. And when I kneel in front of him and tell him to "Look at my eyes," not only does it help him to understand something or help me to get my point across—I think that it does much more than that. It tells William that I am still here, that I love him, and that I'm not going to give up on him. I feel that flame in myself; I'm sure William can see and feel it when he looks at my eyes.

Seth Says...

Don't give up hope.

I don't know if I'll ever have a conversation with my son. I don't know if he'll ever say, "Daddy, where do babies come from?" I don't know if we'll ever have a conversation about hopes and dreams and girls and fears and sports . . . I just don't know.

But I don't give up hope.

And you shouldn't either. We just don't know what might be in store. Think about how far technology has come in our lifetime. I'm a Gen Xer and I can remember when I didn't have to have a phone attached to my head 24/7. I remember when gas was less than one dollar per gallon, music actually came on tapes, and how cool Andrew McCarthy was in *Pretty in Pink*.

And look at us now: high-speed, multimedia, instant results on the Internet . . . and that's been what, ten to fifteen years or less? I graduated college in 1998, and I recall a very few, very select group of students who had cellular phones at the time.

If in twelve years we can go from a phone the size of a briefcase with terrible reception and a charge of $4.50 a minute for a roaming call to what we have now, imagine what will happen with the advancements in testing, therapies, medicine, and diagnostic tools for special-needs children.

And so I will not give up hope. One day my son could say, "Dad, you sure do talk a lot." Or, "You know a few years ago when you were trying to tell me about the Longhorns . . . I really liked hearing about that."

Hey, it could happen. Hang on to that hope.

About the Author

Melanie Fowler has degrees in speech-language pathology and special-education, has worked for years with special-needs and deaf children, and has taught sign language as a second language to high school students. She is also a certified educational diagnostician and has helped children with autism spectrum disorders in groups and on a one-on-one basis. Melanie lives in Texas with her husband, Seth, and their two children, William, age five, and Margaret, age three. This is her first book.